Get Wise

Drugs

➡ what's the danger?

Sarah Medina

Heinemann
LIBRARY

www.heinemann.co.uk/library
Visit our website to find out more information about **Heinemann Library** books.

To order:
☎ Phone 44 (0) 1865 888066
▤ Send a fax to 44 (0) 1865 314091
▯ Visit the Heinemann Bookshop at www.heinemann.co.uk/library to browse our catalogue and order online.

First published in Great Britain by Heinemann Library,
Halley Court, Jordan Hill, Oxford OX2 8EJ, part of Harcourt
Education.

Heinemann is a registered trademark of Harcourt
Education Ltd.

Editorial: Lucy Thunder and Helen Cannons
Design: David Poole and Kamae Design
Illustrations: Jeff Anderson
Picture Research: Rebecca Sodergren and
Kay Altwegg
Production: Edward Moore

Originated by Repro Multi-Warna
Printed in China by WKT Company Limited

The paper used to print this book comes from
sustainable resources.

ISBN 0 431 21004 7
10 9 8 7 6 5 4 3 2 1
08 07 06 05 04

Important note: If you have a
problem relating to drug misuse, go to
the Getting help box on page 31.
There are phone numbers to call for
immediate help and support.

**British Library Cataloguing in
Publication Data**
Medina, Sarah
Drugs – what's the danger?. –
(Get wise)
362.2'9
A full catalogue record for this book is available
from the British Library.

Acknowledgements
The Publishers would like to thank the following for
permission to reproduce photographs: Action Plus p.**11**;
Bubbles p.**15**; Des Conway p.**28**; Corbis/Owen Franken
p.**6**, /Rob Lewine p.**29**, /LWA-Stephen Welstead p.**8**, /RF
p.**16**, /Ariel Skelley p.**4**; Photofusion/Paul Baldesare pp.**7**,
12, **27**, Colin Edwards p.**14**, /G. Montgomery p.**17**, /Ulrika
Preuss p.**23**; PYMCA p.**25**; Science Picture Library/Matt
Meadows and Peter Arnoldine p.**19**; Tudor Photography
pp.**9**, **10**; Janine Wiedel pp.**13**, **20**, **21**, **22**.

Cover photograph of ashtray and bottles reproduced with
permission of Photofusion/Richard Smith.

Quotes and news items are taken from a variety of
sources, including BBC News, BBCi Newsround and the
United Nations Pachamama website.

The Publishers would like to thank Hajra Mir of the
Education and Prevention Team at Drugscope/Alcohol
Concern and John Keast, Principal Manager for Citizenship,
PSHE and RE at the QCA, 1998-2003, for their assistance
in the preparation of this book.

Every effort has been made to contact copyright holders
of any material reproduced in this book. Any omissions
will be rectified in subsequent printings if notice is given
to the Publishers.

Contents

Words appearing in bold, **like this**, are explained in the Glossary.

Drugs all around us

What exactly is a drug – and where are drugs found?

Have you ever taken cough syrup or been given a **painkiller** for a headache? Do you enjoy drinking a cold glass of cola on a hot day, or a hot cup of tea on a cold day? Have you eaten a bar of chocolate today, or this week? If so, you have used drugs! Drugs are a part of all our lives, and many are not harmful if used properly. Other drugs, however, can be extremely bad for your health.

Caffeine

Chocolate, tea, coffee and cola all contain a drug called **caffeine**. Caffeine can give you a 'buzz' and a short burst of energy. Caffeine can sometimes be dangerous. Too much is bad for you – it can make your heart race, and can make you feel nervous and jumpy.

Soft drinks such as cola may be just what you fancy – but too much of the caffeine they contain is bad for your health. ➲

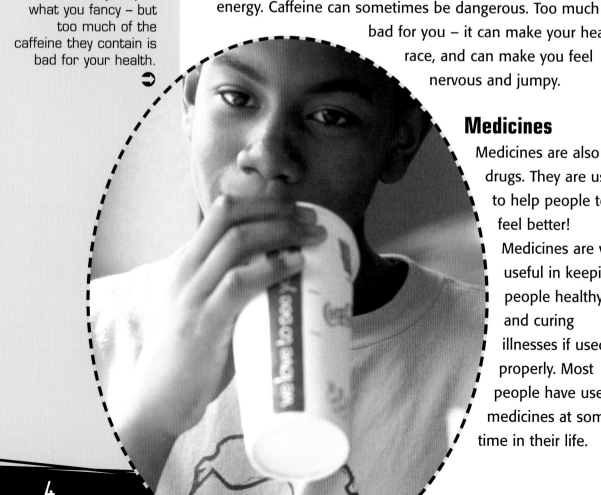

Medicines

Medicines are also drugs. They are used to help people to feel better! Medicines are very useful in keeping people healthy and curing illnesses if used properly. Most people have used medicines at some time in their life.

Alcohol and tobacco

You have probably seen people smoking cigarettes or drinking **alcohol**. Cigarettes are made from **tobacco**, which contains a powerful drug called **nicotine**. Nicotine helps people to unwind and feel more relaxed. People drink alcohol – such as beer, wine and vodka – to relax and have fun, too. Although, in most countries, these drugs are found everywhere, it does not mean that they are safe. It is **legal** to sell these drugs, but only to people over a certain age.

Illegal drugs

Some drugs, such as **cannabis**, are **illegal**. It is against the law to use them. Selling certain products – mainly **volatile substances** – for use as drugs is also illegal. You may also have heard of illegal drugs called Ecstasy, cocaine and heroin. These drugs are dangerous, and people could get into a lot of trouble with the police for selling and using them.

The right choice

This book will help you to find out about some of the different kinds of drugs. You will discover what they are, why people use them – and the dangers involved. You will also learn how to say 'No' to drug misuse which is the right choice, every time.

Our home is a drug free zone!

What are the risks of using drugs?

In many countries, people are using drugs more than ever before. Strong coffee keeps them going during the day, **alcohol** and cigarettes help them to relax at night, and they take medicines at the slightest hint of feeling ill. More people are turning to **illegal** drugs, too.

Safe drugs, dangerous drugs

Many drugs – for example, **caffeine** and medicines – are usually safe, if used properly. Some drugs – such as alcohol and **tobacco** – are not so safe, and it is only **legal** for older people to buy them. Even then, they have to be used with care. Other drugs are illegal, and using them has many risks – particularly to a person's health.

➡ Sometimes friends or other people try to give away or sell drugs in the school playground. Learning about drugs can help you to know why you should say 'no'.

Drug abuse

Drug **abuse** is when people use drugs in a harmful way. All sorts of people from all sorts of families **misuse** drugs. Some adults abuse alcohol by drinking too much. Children sometimes smoke cigarettes when they are very young. People of all ages abuse illegal drugs, such as **cannabis**. Some people start misusing drugs while they are still at school.

Drug addiction

If used very carefully, some drugs may not cause much harm. But drugs can also be dangerous, and people can become **addicted** to them. People who are addicted find that they cannot stop using them, even if they want to. They are **dependent** on the drug, and they will do anything – even steal, or hurt people – to get more. Their lives start to fall apart, bit by bit.

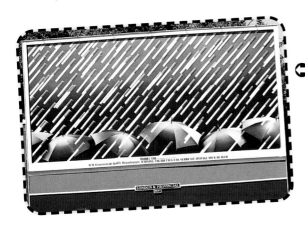

◀ Cigarette advertisements encourage people to smoke – and so the governments in the UK and Australia have banned them.

Talk time

Why do you think that some young people use drugs?

Tyrone: Perhaps they don't realize the possible dangers of drugs.

ali: There can be a lot of pressure to use drugs, too.

Maribel: If everyone else is doing it, it can be hard to say no, especially if you're curious.

Lauren: And you often see people on TV drinking and smoking.

ali: Yeah, and that makes it seem normal and safe.

Newsflash

In the UK, Prince Harry admitted that he smoked cannabis and drank heavily when he was sixteen. After the truth came out, his father, Prince Charles, took him to spend a day at a special clinic that helps people who are addicted to very bad drugs. The experience helped Harry to think much more carefully about the dangers of drugs.

Take your medicine

What are medicines – and why do we need them?

◑ Many people depend on their medicine to control an ongoing illness. This girl is using an inhaler to control the breathing disease, asthma.

Medicines are drugs that help people to feel better when they are ill. They are **legal** if used properly by the person they are intended for, but they can be dangerous if they are not used with proper care. You can buy some kinds of medicines, such as cough medicine, in shops and supermarkets. For most kinds, you need to get a **prescription** from your doctor, which you normally take to a pharmacy to exchange for the medicine you need.

What for?

Medicines are very important. They are used for various reasons. They can help people to get better from an illness – or to help them to feel more comfortable whilst they are ill. They can also be used to stop someone from getting ill in the first place. And, if someone has an ongoing illness, medicines can be used to control their **symptoms** on a day-to-day basis.

Talk time

What kinds of medicines have you used?

 ali: My mum has given me cough medicine before.

Maribel: Mine gives me vitamins to try to stop me from catching a cold.

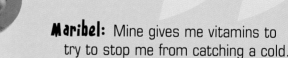 **Lauren:** My dad gave me a **painkiller** when I had a headache.

Tyrone: When I had a really bad sore throat, I had to take **antibiotics**.

 ali: When we were little, we all had **vaccinations**, too.

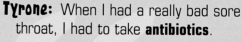

Pills and potions

Just go into a pharmacy, and look at all the rows of tablets, creams, syrups, drops and sprays! These are all different types of medicine. Medicines can also come as an injection – or even as a gas. Medicines come in many different forms, and people use them a lot. New medicines, in new forms, are being created by drug companies all the time.

◖ Medicines come in many different forms, shapes and sizes – some of them specially designed so they can be taken easily.

THINK IT THROUGH

Do we depend too much on medicines?

Yes. People take medicines as soon as they feel even a little bit ill. They don't give their body a chance to fight the illness naturally.

No. If we didn't have medicines, many people would die of illnesses unnecessarily.

What do YOU think?

One pill too many?

Can using medicines ever be dangerous, or wrong?

Medicines do a great job in preventing and treating illness. But all drugs, including medicines, can be dangerous if they are not used properly. Sometimes, people – including sports people – **abuse** medicines, and get themselves into all sorts of difficulty.

Fact Flash

In the year 2000, doctors in England gave out 552 million prescriptions – almost 11 prescriptions for each person.

Wrong dose

All medicines should be taken with care. It can be dangerous to use medicines that are not for you, or if you do not need them for an illness. If you take the medicine in the wrong way – for example, if you take the wrong amount at the wrong time – it will not help you, and could even harm you.

TOP TIPS

Follow these top tips for using medicines safely:

◎ Only ever take a medicine given to you by a doctor, parent or carer.

◎ Always take the exact amount you need, and for as long as you have been told to.

◎ Take it the way you should – for example, by mouth.

◎ Make a note of when you take it, so you can check this later.

◎ Watch out for side effects, such as a rash.

◎ Make sure that medicines are stored safely – out of the reach of small children.

◎ Let an adult know you are taking your medicine.

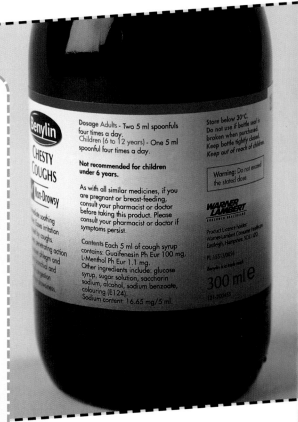

↻ Be safe – always follow the directions and take your medicine properly.

Addiction

Some people become **addicted** to medicines – for example, to strong **painkillers** given on **prescription** by a doctor – especially if they have to use them for a long time. Their body and mind become so used to the medicine that they are **dependent** on it and cannot live a normal life without it. Fortunately, with help from their doctor, family and friends, people can break their addiction.

Drugs in sport

Recently, drug abuse has become more common in sports. Some sports people take medicines, such as **anabolic steroids**, to make them perform better. Special tests to check whether sports people have used drugs are helping to stop this problem. If people are found to have used a drug which is **illegal** in their sport, they can be **banned** from taking part in the sport.

◑ Tests to check whether players have used drugs illegally are common in many sports, including football.

Newsflash

Top Australian cricketer Shane Warne was banned from playing cricket for a year after tests in 2003 showed that he had used a medicine, called a diuretic, which is banned in cricket under anti-drug rules. A diuretic makes your body release more water (you go to the toilet a lot), and is banned in sport because it can be used to flush out proof of using other drugs.

THINK IT THROUGH

Is it wrong for sports people to use drugs?

Yes. Drugs give sports people an unfair advantage over others – and they may be harming themselves, too.

No. There is always pressure for them to do better – and drugs may help them. The most important thing is winning.

What do YOU think?

Just a tipple

What is alcohol, and why is it so popular?

'Having a tipple' – meaning having an **alcoholic drink** – is a popular pastime in many countries. In countries such as the the UK and Australia, people enjoy drinking in pubs and at home to relax and have fun.

Fact Flash

Women should not drink more than two to three 'units' of alcohol a day. Men should not drink more than three to four units a day. Two units equals half a can of strong lager.

Drinking poison

Have you ever heard the expression, 'What's your poison?' It is a way of asking what a person's favourite alcoholic drink is! Alcohol contains a poisonous drug called **ethanol**. Spirits, such as vodka and whisky, contain more alcohol than other drinks, such as beer and **alcopops**. The more alcohol a drink contains, the faster it will make a person drunk.

Getting drunk

When people drink just a little alcohol, they feel more relaxed, confident and happy. As they drink more alcohol, other, less pleasant effects kick in. They find it hard to speak clearly, they get clumsy and they can feel very emotional. They are much more likely than usual to have an accident. People who are drunk can become very tearful, or loud and aggressive. And, as their body tries to get rid of the poisonous ethanol, they may be physically sick.

➲ Alcopops may look and taste similar to soft drinks, but they can make you drunk quickly – which can be very dangerous.

Starting young

Do you know anyone at school who has drunk alcohol? People are starting to drink it at a younger and younger age – even though it is very bad for their health. The younger you are, the more the alcohol affects you, because your body is smaller and it cannot cope with the ethanol as easily.

Talk time

Why do you think young people start drinking alcohol?

Lauren: Some people think it's cool and grown-up.

Tyrone: And they drink because their friends are drinking, or because they see people drinking on TV.

ali: Sometimes, they're just bored or unhappy.

Maribel: Yeah, drinking might make them feel happier and more confident for a while – but it doesn't last.

THINK IT THROUGH

Should parents allow young people to drink at home?

Yes. That way, they can learn to drink sensibly and safely.

No. It can make drinking seem normal, and then they will just drink more.

What do YOU think?

Newsflash

Some UK parents may encourage their children to drink. According to a 2001 study, one in four eleven-year-old boys and one in six girls have at least one alcoholic drink a week. Many of the children said they had alcohol for the first time at home or at family occasions, such as weddings, and then started drinking quite often. The study shocked experts, who say it is up to parents to set a good example with alcohol at home.

🎧 People drink to relax – but drinking too much is bad for your health.

What are the dangers of drinking alcohol?

People often drink **alcohol** to 'chill out', but drinking too much can have the opposite effect – it can ruin your fun! Even worse, it can ruin your health.

The flipside

So – people think that drinking a lot of alcohol is fun? Well, here is the flipside. Drinking too much, and drinking when you are too young, causes problem after problem. People who are drunk lose control over their mind and body. They are more likely to get into arguments or fights, or to have accidents. They can feel miserable, because alcohol affects their mood.

Top thoughts

'I've seen people drunk – and it's not attractive.'

Justin Timberlake, pop star

People who drink ➜ too much may need to be treated in hospital for alcohol poisoning.

When people drink too much, their body cannot get rid of the poisonous **ethanol** fast enough. It stays in their blood, making them feel very ill. They may vomit, or even collapse. They may have to be rushed to hospital with **alcohol poisoning**. When the effects of the alcohol wear off, they will have an unpleasant **hangover**, which can last for up to two days.

Alcohol addiction

People who drink a lot of alcohol for a long period of time can become **addicted** to it. **Alcoholics** can lose their friends and family – and their health, too. They can get brain damage, liver damage, heart problems and other serious illnesses, such as **cancer**, which can kill them.

Alcohol and the law

Because alcohol can be dangerous, there are **laws** to protect young people from its effects. In the UK, young people are allowed to drink beer or cider with a meal in a restaurant when they are sixteen years old, but it is **illegal** for them to buy alcohol until they are eighteen. If they are caught drinking in a public place below that age, they can get into trouble with the police and the alcohol will be taken away.

In many countries, such as the UK and ➲ Australia, young people cannot buy alcohol until they are eighteen years old. In the USA, they have to be 21.

TOP TIPS

Follow these top tips to help you to say 'No!' to underage drinking:

◎ Remember – no one can make you do anything you don't want to.

◎ Be clear about your decision. Say 'No' politely, but firmly. You don't need to make excuses.

◎ Stay away from situations where you might be pressurized to do something you don't want to.

◎ Try to choose friends who think like you and share your interests.

THINK IT THROUGH

Given the risks, should people drink alcohol at all?

Yes. As long as people keep their drinking under control, it is fine.

No. It is not worth risking damaging their health or getting addicted.

What do YOU think?

A puff of smoke

What makes smoking cigarettes so tempting?

Fact Flash

In the UK, 450 children start smoking every day. Some children as young as five years old are regular smokers.

People have been smoking cigarettes for more than 100 years. For a long time, people did not know about the dangers of smoking. Nowadays, most people are well aware that smoking is bad news – and yet many still carry on.

What are cigarettes?

Cigarettes are made using **tobacco**, which contains a very **addictive** drug called **nicotine**. Cigarettes also contain thousands of other nasty substances, including **carbon monoxide** and **tar**. When someone puffs on a cigarette, they breathe these substances through their mouth and throat into their lungs.

Who smokes?

About one-third of all adults in the UK and Australia smoke cigarettes. Most adult smokers started smoking when they were teenagers, and then found it hard to give up. Although the number of smokers is falling gradually, smoking is still a serious problem in many countries – and too many young people still start to smoke and get addicted.

Cigarettes are made ➲ from tobacco plants. You may think they are natural, but each cigarette contains 4000 harmful chemicals.

Just one more...

Nicotine is very addictive. People who smoke often say that cigarettes make them feel calmer and happier – but this only lasts for a short while and, in the end, they have to smoke another cigarette to feel like that again! Really, they are just addicted – which causes them to make up all sorts of excuses so they can continue to smoke.

Passive smoking

Most people who smoke, choose to smoke. Unfortunately, every time they have a cigarette, other people are affected, too. 'Passive smoking' is the term used for breathing in the nasty substances released by someone else's cigarette. It can make the non-smoker ill, through no fault of their own.

Newsflash

There may be lots of reasons why people start smoking, but stopping can be hard. Researchers say that young people are more at risk of becoming addicted because their brains are still developing. They found that girls who smoke occasionally become addicted after smoking for three weeks, and boys get hooked after about six months.

Talk time

What makes young people smoke?

 ali: Lots of people think it will impress their friends and that it looks cool.

Lauren: People whose family smoke often think smoking's an OK thing to do.

 Tyrone: Yes, but sometimes people start smoking to be rebellious, too.

Maribeli: After a while, smoking just becomes a habit – people get hooked.

Most smokers wish that they ➲ could stop smoking. The best thing is not to start in the first place!

What makes smoking so dangerous?

It is a fact: smoking can make you ill – and even kill you. Half of all the people who smoke for years will die because of it. And yet people still do it! Let's look at some of the effects of cigarettes.

The ashtray effect

Have you ever been around someone who smokes? Have you noticed that their hair and their clothes smell? Some people say that smokers smell like an ashtray! It may not sound very nice – but they do have a point. If people smoke a lot, their fingers can become stained yellow, too.

More seriously, smoking affects people's lungs. People who smoke find they cannot do sports as well as they did before they smoked. They may get out of breath just running for the bus.

Fact Flash

Every day in the UK, about 300 people die younger than they should do because of smoking.

Smoky Nights

Risking life

Cigarettes contain thousands of poisonous substances, including **nicotine**, **carbon monoxide** and **tar**. Breathing in these substances can give people life-threatening illnesses, such as **cancer** and **heart disease**. Smoking can also affect the way that blood travels around the body – and 2000 people a year in the UK have to have an arm or a leg removed because of this.

Cigarettes and the law

It is **illegal** to sell cigarettes to young people under the age of sixteen. Shopkeepers who knowingly sell cigarettes to underage smokers can get into trouble with the police. In 2003, the UK government decided to **ban** cigarette advertising, because they know that it encourages people to smoke. Australia has banned cigarette advertising for the same reason. In many countries, it is also illegal to smoke in some public places.

TOP TIPS

It is easy to avoid all the nasty side effects of smoking – don't start smoking in the first place! See the 'Top tips' on page 15 to help you to say 'No!'.

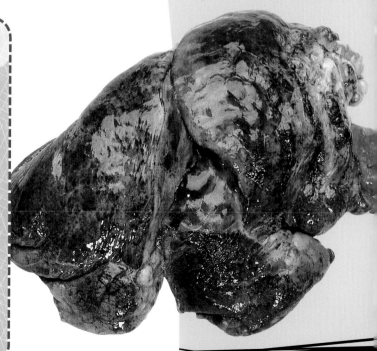

❶ Smokers damage their lungs. Healthy lungs should be pink. Instead, these unhealthy lungs belonging to a smoker have turned black from years of breathing in poisonous smoke.

THINK IT THROUGH

Is it OK to smoke, even though it is dangerous?

Yes. It's up to me if I want to smoke. People can keep away if they don't like it.

No. It's too easy to get hooked – and it's really hard to stop. Your health really suffers.

What do YOU think?

What are volatile substances – and what makes people use them?

Do you use glue at home or school? Did you know that some people use glue as a drug? Some everyday products, such as glue and air fresheners, are called **volatile substances**, and they can be **abused**. Abusing volatile substances can be very dangerous indeed.

Breathing it in

People who abuse volatile substances often breathe, or 'sniff', them into their lungs through a cloth or sleeve. Sometimes, they squirt gas products into the back of their throat. Doing this makes them feel as if they are very drunk. They may become dizzy, dreamy and giggly, and have **hallucinations** – but only for a short time. To keep up these effects, they have to keep coming back for more.

Danger zone!

Abusing volatile substances is very risky. It makes people feel very tired and sick – and some people collapse. People may choke to death, and also get life-threatening heart problems from doing it. People who have just used volatile substances can hurt themselves, may not recognize dangers and can take risks they would not normally take. Abusing volatile substances makes people look bad, too – their skin gets pale and spotty, and their eyes can look red.

Volatile substances are common products that release fumes when they are used. People who abuse them put themselves at risk of harm.

Volatile substances and the law

Because many volatile substances are common products, it is not possible to make them **illegal**. However, in the UK and Australia, it is illegal for shopkeepers to sell these products to people under the age of eighteen if they believe that the products will be abused.

Some people sniff volatile substances through a paper bag or with a plastic bag over their head. This can suffocate and kill them. *Do not do this – ever!*

THINK IT THROUGH

Should products that can be used as volatile substances carry a health warning?

Yes. People may not know the possible risks, and so they should be warned.

No. It won't stop people who want to from abusing them – and it might give them ideas, instead.

What do YOU think?

Cannabis

Why do some people use cannabis and why is it risky?

Cannabis is the most commonly used **illegal** drug in the UK and Australia. People of all ages use it – some as young as eleven years old. Some people say that cannabis is safer than cigarettes or **alcohol** – but, like all drugs, cannabis can cause a lot of harm.

Just another plant?

Cannabis is made from a plant called hemp. People often smoke cannabis mixed with **tobacco** in a kind of cigarette called a 'joint' or a 'spliff'. Others smoke it on its own in a special pipe. Some people cook and eat it. Cannabis has many other names, including blow, draw, ganja, hash, marijuana, puff, skunk, wacky-backy or weed.

Cannabis leaves are 🔼 made into different forms, which can be smoked or eaten.

Getting stoned

When people use cannabis, they can feel very relaxed and friendly. Everything can look and sound clearer – even colours can seem brighter. This is called being 'stoned'. However, this is just the effect of the drug and, when the effects wear off, they may feel very differently indeed.

Cannabis risks

When people are stoned, they are much more likely to have an accident. If they are feeling unhappy when they use cannabis, they may soon feel worse – even panicky and afraid. These feelings may carry on, even after the effects of the cannabis have worn off.

Using cannabis also causes many health problems. People who use cannabis regularly may find that their brain does not work as well as it used to – it can be hard to concentrate, and their memory often gets worse. Cannabis causes lung damage, too, and can lead to lung **cancer**. If people have heart problems, cannabis can make them worse.

Although cannabis is not physically **addictive**, many people who use cannabis find it very hard to stop using it. Regular cannabis users can feel as if they do not have any energy. It can be difficult for them to get on with everyday things.

Cannabis and the law

Cannabis is an illegal drug. If the police find someone using it, or even just carrying it, they can get into trouble. People can even be sent to court for possession of cannabis.

Young people are using cannabis despite the risks, according to one study. Almost a third of all boys and a quarter of all girls aged fourteen and fifteen admitted using the drug. The study also found that young people think that cannabis isn't 'always unsafe'. But scientists say that just one cannabis cigarette has the same amount of cancer-causing chemicals in it as five ordinary cigarettes.

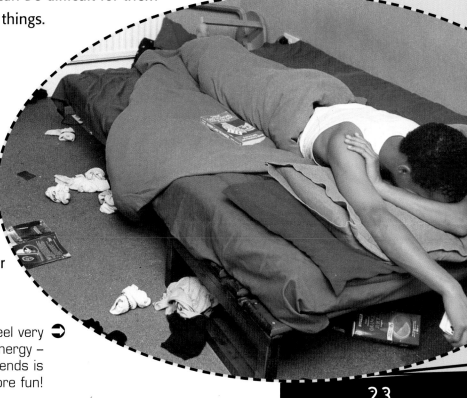

Cannabis can make you feel very ➲ tired. Don't waste your energy – playing sport with your friends is much more fun!

What is it like to be addicted to drugs?

Do you know someone who can't give up chocolate or coffee, even if they want to? All drugs – even **legal** drugs – can be **addictive**. Most people who use drugs think that they will never become **addicted**, but addiction is a very real risk from drug **abuse** – and addiction ruins lives.

Types of addiction

No one who uses drugs ever plans to become addicted but, before they know it, they can be trapped. Some drugs – such as **alcohol** – are 'physically' addictive, which means that the person's body comes to depend on the drug to work properly. Some other drugs – such as **cannabis** – are 'psychologically' addictive. This means that people get so used to the feeling they get from using it that they crave it more and more.

Talk time

What kinds of things might addicts do to get drugs?

Tyrone: They would usually do things that can get them money to pay for more drugs.

Maribel: They might borrow money from their family or mates, and never pay it back.

Lauren: Or they might start stealing or shoplifting.

ali: Yeah, and then they sell the stuff they steal to get money.

Tyrone: Sometimes, drug addicts even attack people to steal their money.

Life of an addict

If someone is addicted to a drug, they may notice that they think about it a great deal, or that they will do anything to use it as much as possible. They may do this in secret, or they may hang around other drug users. They may get very angry if anyone tries to talk to them about the problem. They lie to the people they love, because the drug becomes more important than anything or anyone.

As their addiction gets worse, their life falls apart. Their relationships with family and friends often suffer – and so does their health. They find it hard to study or work. And, because buying drugs can be expensive, they may even get involved with crime, such as stealing.

Getting help

If someone you know is addicted to drugs, they need to get help as quickly as possible. It could even save their life. Page 26 gives lots of ideas for giving and getting help.

Some drugs are so dangerous that they can make you really ill – and even kill you.

THINK IT THROUGH

Do people who are addicted to drugs know how much they are harming themselves?

Yes. They usually know that they are in trouble, but they often can't see a way out.

No. They are so trapped that they can't see what is happening to them. All they think about is the drug.

What do YOU think?

Help at hand

If someone has a problem with drugs, where can they go to get help?

People who **abuse** drugs – medicines, **alcohol**, cigarettes, **volatile substances** or **cannabis** – can, and do, manage to stop. Even people who are **addicted** to drugs can quit. The important thing is to get help. Fortunately, there is a lot of support available for those who need it.

Time to quit

Drugs can kill. People who abuse drugs need to stop. It can be hard for someone to own up to having a drugs problem – even to themselves. They need to be very honest and brave. But, as soon as they do face the facts, they have taken the first step on the path to recovery. The next step is to get help and support from people they trust.

TOP TIPS

If you think that you may have a problem with drugs – or if you know someone else who does – it will really help you to talk about it to someone you trust. This may seem difficult, but you can do it! Follow these top tips for getting started:

◎ It can help to practise what you want to say in advance. Try writing it down first.

◎ Remember to tell the whole story – which drug or drugs you/they are using, when you started, how often you do it, and what effect it is having on you.

◎ Be prepared to speak out clearly if the person you speak to suggests doing something that you think will make things worse. Work it out together.

A friend in need

As the saying goes, 'A friend in need is a friend indeed.' If you know someone who has problems with drugs, you can try to be a good friend to them – and let them know that they are not alone. If you are not sure what to do or say, you could talk to someone you trust – such as a carer or a teacher.

Getting help

People who are **misusing** drugs, and who want to quit, need lots of help and support from someone they can trust who knows something about drugs. This could be a parent, an older brother or sister, a teacher, a school counsellor or youth club leader, a doctor, or an experienced support worker at a drugs information centre or helpline. Page 31 has a list of organizations that help people with different types of drug problems.

⊙ Doctors can help people who have drug problems to overcome them, step by step.

THINK IT THROUGH

Do you think that people who have a problem with drugs should get help from others?

No. People who use drugs usually get themselves into the problem – and so they should get themselves out of it.

Yes. People never mean to get into problems with drugs. Because drugs can be very addictive, it is too hard for people to deal with it alone – they need help.

What do YOU think?

What's the right choice when it comes to drugs?

People are using drugs at a younger and younger age. You may know someone at school who has tried **alcohol** or cigarettes. Perhaps you have even been offered these drugs yourself. How do you make the right choice if someone offers you drugs?

Yes or no?

If people use drugs, they risk **addiction**, illness and many other problems. It might be hard to say 'No' to drugs, especially if everyone else is using them, but saying 'No' will keep you safer, healthier – and happier. It may be your choice – but only one choice is the right choice.

🎧 Lots of people abuse drugs – but many, many more do not. It is always possible to enjoy yourself with friends without alcohol or drugs.

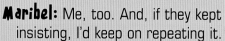

Talk time

What would you do if someone offered you a cigarette or a bottle of alcopop?

ali: I would just say, 'No, thanks.'

Maribel: Me, too. And, if they kept insisting, I'd keep on repeating it.

Tyrone: I'd make sure I sounded really clear when I said 'No' – otherwise they might think that I didn't mean it.

Lauren: I'd probably change the subject, as if I hadn't heard them. Or I'd just walk away.

Know your stuff

One of the best ways you can help yourself to make the right choice about drugs is to learn about them – what they are, why people use them and the risks involved. Reading this book is a great start. Check out some of the other books and websites mentioned on page 31, too. Knowing your stuff will help you to say 'No' to drugs loudly and clearly – and to stick to your decision.

What's the alternative?

Some young people claim that life is boring – and so they use drugs to 'spice things up'. Remember – there are far better things to do to make life more interesting than smoking, getting drunk or sniffing glue. Try playing a sport, spending time on a favourite hobby, listening to music, playing games or watching a film. Think about what you really like to do – and then get started!

You can have lots of fun without drugs. ➲
Doing an activity that you like can help
you stay healthy and happy, too.

Top thoughts

'Drugs? Everyone has a choice, and I choose not to do drugs.'

Leonardo DiCaprio,
US actor

THINK IT THROUGH

Shouldn't people be allowed to use all kinds of drugs, if they want to?

Yes. They may just want to have fun – and they might be prepared to take the risks that go with the drugs.

No. Drugs are far too dangerous for people to mess about with. There are many other things people can do to have fun without risking their mental and physical health.

What do YOU think?

abuse when something is used in a wrong or dangerous way, or illegally

addicted/addiction when it is hard to stop doing something, because either your mind or your body has got so used to it that it needs it to feel normal

addictive when something causes an addition

alcohol/alcoholic drink type of drink that can make people drunk because it contains a drug called ethanol. Alcoholic drinks include wine, beer, cider, alcopops and vodka.

alcoholic someone addicted to alcohol

alcohol poisoning effects of drinking too much alcohol, causing vomiting or collapse. Alcohol poisoning needs treatment in a hospital.

alcopop type of alcoholic drink that looks and tastes like a soft drink, but contains a lot of alcohol. Alcopops are especially made to attract young people.

anabolic steroid medicine sometimes used to treat illnesses related to the blood and growth. Anabolic steroids are sometimes abused by sports people who want to improve their performance.

antibiotic medicine that fights bacterial infections. Penicillin is an antibiotic.

ban when something is officially forbidden (by the government)

caffeine drug found in coffee, tea, chocolate and soft drinks, such as cola

cancer illness caused when tiny cells in the body grow and spread very quickly

cannabis drug made from a plant called hemp. People smoke or eat cannabis.

carbon monoxide poisonous fumes in cigarette smoke. Carbon monoxide is also released in car exhaust causing air pollution.

dependent when your body has become so used to something that it needs it to feel normal

epidemic illness that spreads quickly

ethanol drug found in alcoholic drinks such as beer, wine, cider and vodka

hallucination when your brain doesn't work properly and causes you to see things that are not really there

hangover after-effect of drinking too much alcohol. A person with a hangover may get a bad headache, sore eyes and a dry mouth, and feel sick.

heart disease when the heart does not work properly

illegal against the law. People who do illegal things can get into trouble with the police.

law rule or set of rules that a whole community or country has to follow

legal something the law allows

misuse using something in an illegal, dangerous or abusive way

nicotine highly addictive drug found in tobacco products, such as cigarettes

painkiller medicine that stops pain, such as a headache

prescription instruction from a doctor telling a chemist to provide someone with a particular medicine

symptoms particular signs or problems brought on by an illness or disease

tar thick, sticky black substance produced by burning tobacco in cigarettes

tobacco dried leaves of the tobacco plant, used to make cigarettes

vaccination medicine given to prevent certain illnesses, such as measles

volatile substance chemical substance (also known as a solvent or inhalant) that releases vapour, which people use as a drug

Check it out

Check out these books and websites to find out more about different types of drugs, and where to get help and advice.

Books

Health Matters: Drugs and Your Health, Jillian Powell (Wayland, 1997)

Learn to Say No: Alcohol/Smoking/Cannabis/Solvents (four books), Angela Royston (Heinemann Library, 2001)

Viewpoints: Drug Abuse, Emma Haughton (Franklin Watts, 2001)

Organizations to help people with drug problems

Australian Drug Foundation (Australia): www.adf.org.au

ChildLine (UK): www.childline.org.uk tel. 0800 1111

Drinkline (UK): tel. 0800 917 8282

Kids Against Tobacco Smoke (UK): www.roycastle.org/kats

Kids Helpline (Australia): www.kidshelp.com.au
  tel. 1800 55 1800

Kidscape (UK): www.kidscape.org.uk tel. 08451 205 204

LifeBytes (UK): www.lifebytes.gov.uk

FRANK Helpline (UK): www.talktofrank.com
  tel. 0800 77 66 00

Re-Solv (inhalant abuse UK): www.re-solv.org tel. 0808 800 2345

The Centre for Recovery (UK): www.recovery.org.uk

Think About Drink (UK): www.wrecked.co.uk

Getting help

If you feel very worried or upset about a drug problem, you may want to talk to someone urgently. You can speak to an adult you trust, or phone a helpline for support.

• In the UK, you can phone FRANK helpline on 0800 77 66 00 (open 24 hours a day). Please remember that calls to 0800 numbers are free, and they do not show up on phone bills.

• In Australia, you can phone Kids Help Line on 1800 55 1800 (open 24 hours a day).

Remember – you do not have to be alone.

Index

Titles in the *Get Wise* series:

Hardback 0 431 21003 9

Hardback 0 431 21004 7

Hardback 0 431 21002 0

Hardback 0 431 21000 4

Hardback 0 431 21001 2

Find out about other Heinemann library titles on our website www.heinemann.co.uk/library